Fire Department

AMBULANCE

AIRCRAFT
RESCUE

FIRE DEPARTMENT

FIRE & RESCUE

OIL SPILL
RECOVERY

DISASTER RELIEF TEAM

OPERATIONAL COMMAND
FIRE & RESCUE

FIRE & RESCUE

Edition 2019


Bauernstr. 11d
DE-86391 Stadtbergen
Germany

Made in the USA
Las Vegas, NV
08 May 2024

89666118R00037